Old Testament Tales

from The Lion Storyteller Bible

Retold by Bob Hartman

Illustrations by Susie Poole

LION
Children's Books

Text copyright © 1995 Bob Hartman
Illustrations copyright © 1995 Susie Poole
This edition copyright © 2000 Lion Publishing

The moral rights of the author and illustrator
have been asserted

Published by
Lion Publishing plc
Sandy Lane West, Oxford, England
www.lion-publishing.co.uk
ISBN 0 7459 4407 8

First edition 2000
10 9 8 7 6 5 4 3 2 1 0

A catalogue record for this book is available
from the British Library

Printed and bound in Spain

Contents

In the Beginning

At first, there wasn't anything at all. Nothing! So God set to work. But he didn't use his hands, or a special machine. He spoke, that's all. He said, 'I'd like some light.' And there was light. Brighter than a summer morning or a thousand Christmas candles.

God spoke again. He said, 'Sky. I'd like some sky. And some water underneath.' And, sure enough, there it was. The bright blue sky. With the dark blue heavens above it. And the blue-green sea below.

'Earth.' That's what God said next, hard and firm, as if he really meant it. And the blue-green waters parted, and there was dry land underneath. Great patches of it, dirt black and brown. Here and there, all over the world.

'We need some colour,' God whispered, as if he were thinking out loud. And, quivering with excitement, green growing things crept right up out of the dark earth, then burst into blossom—red, orange and blue! Pine trees and palm trees. Rose bushes and blackberry bushes. Tulips and chrysanthemums.

God shouted next.
'Day—shining sun!'
'Night—shining moon!'
'Bright shining stars!'

And there they were, for morning and evening, summer and winter—time and heat and light!

After that, God called to the sky, as if he were expecting some kind of an answer.

'Come forth, flying things!' he called.

And through the clouds they came. Flying high and flying low. Flying large and flying small. Eagles and insects. Hummingbirds and hawks.

Then God called to the sea.

'Come forth, splashing things!'

And they came to him, too, leaping right up through the waves. Sailfish and swordfish. Dolphins and trout. Great grinning hump-backed whales.

Finally, God called to the earth.

'Come forth, walking things, crawling things, running, hopping, climbing things!'

And sure enough, they came. Up from burrows. Down from trees. Out of the high grass, and across the open plains.

Now everything was ready. Good and ready. So God spoke again.

'Man and woman,' is what he said, as if he were calling the names of his very best friends.

And out of the dust came Adam and Eve. To enjoy all that God had made. To take care of it for him. And to talk with him.

'This is the way things ought to be,' God said at last. 'This is good!'

A Special Promise

God was sad. Very sad. Everywhere he looked, he saw people making bad choices. Hating each other. Hurting each other. Making a mess of his beautiful world.

'I need to start all over again,' God decided. 'I need to make my world clean.' And that's when he talked to Noah.

Noah was not like the rest. He was a good man, and God knew it. So God told him to build a boat. A boat big enough to hold:

Noah,

his wife,

his three sons,

their wives,

a pair of every animal in the world,

and food enough to feed all of them for a very long time!

Noah's family was surprised when he told them what he was going to do.

Noah's neighbours thought it strange of him to build a boat so far from the sea.

And it wasn't easy chasing, and catching, and cleaning up after all those animals.

But Noah was a good man. He did what God told him—even when it was hard.

At last, when they were all tucked safely away in the boat, God shut the door. And then it started to rain.

It rained for forty days.

It rained for forty nights.

It rained harder than Noah had ever seen it rain before.

It rained so hard that the streams, and the rivers, and even the seas burst their banks and began to flood. Soon every sandy beach, every rocky path, every patch of muddy earth had disappeared beneath the water.

And the boat began to float.

It floated above the houses. It floated above the trees. It floated above the hills, and then above the mountains, too.

It floated for days and weeks and months.

And then it stopped, stuck at the top of a tall mountain.

Noah opened a window to look out. The water was going down, but the world was far from dry.

So he sent out a dove. And when the dove did not come back, Noah knew that it had found a dry place to build its nest.

'Come out!' God called, finally. 'Come out of the boat! The world is dry. The world is clean. And now you and your family and all the animals must have children and fill it full of life again!'

'Hooray!' Noah celebrated. And he thanked God for saving him.

God was happy, too. So he painted the world's first rainbow in the sky—to celebrate his fresh, clean world. And to promise that he would never send a flood like that again.

The Tall Tower

God looked. Something was happening in the land of Shinar.

God listened. And this is what he heard:

'Hey, you,' called a tall man. 'Throw me a brick.'

'Here you go,' snorted a short man, 'and could you pass me that axe?'

From all over the world, they had come— tall people, short people, fat people, thin people, all kinds of people. And they were building a tower!

Up, up, up they went. Stirring mortar. Making bricks. And hauling them high into the sky.

It was a big job. It was hard work. So it was a good thing they all spoke the same language—at least they could understand each other.

God looked and God listened again. This is what he heard:

'Say,' asked a fat man, 'why are we building this tower, anyway?'

'It's simple,' grinned a thin man. 'When we are finished this will be the tallest tower in the whole world.

'People will pass by, look at it and be amazed. We'll be more famous than the greatest king. We'll be more important than God himself!'

Now when God heard that, he jumped! And then he smiled.

'More important than me?' he chuckled. 'We'll see about that.'

That's when God decided to play the world's first trick. Did he wave his hand? Did he say some special words? Or did he just think it into happening? No one knows. But the next time God listened, this is what he heard:

'Hey, you,' called the tall man, 'pass me some mortar.'

'Fortwort?' snorted the short man. 'Hort mort a bortle.' (Which means something like, 'What did you say? I can't understand you.')

God chuckled again. He was enjoying this. So he listened some more.

'Excuse me,' asked the fat man, 'could I borrow your hammer?'

But the thin man didn't have a clue what he meant. 'Hub-wub?' he said. 'Flub-bub-a-gubble.' (Which means something like, 'What?')

And so it was, all over the tower. Instead of one language, there were suddenly hundreds. The workers couldn't understand each other. How could they go on?

So down, down, down they climbed, dropping their tools as they went. Then they babbled off in every direction, leaving the tower half-finished, half-done.

And whenever people passed by they were not amazed. No, some sniggered, some pointed, and some even said, 'Flep-nepp. Shlepp-rep-a-zepp.' (Which means something like, 'See, those men weren't more important than God, after all.')

Joseph the Dreamer

Jacob had twelve sons. That's right—twelve!

His favourite son was Joseph. Jacob spoiled him and gave him special gifts—like a beautiful coat decorated with many colours.

Reds and greens. Blues and yellows. Purples and pinks. Joseph was bright as a rainbow and proud as a peacock.

Joseph's older brothers did not like this one bit. But what they hated even more were Joseph's dreams!

'I had a dream last night,' boasted Joseph.

'Oh no,' groaned his brothers.

'I dreamed that we were all bundles of wheat. And guess what happened? Your bundles of wheat bowed down and worshipped mine!'

'And I had another dream,' Joseph bragged.

'Go on,' his brothers sighed.

'I dreamed we were all stars. And guess what? Your stars bowed down to mine, just as if I were your king!'

It didn't take long for Joseph's brothers to grow tired of this. But that's no excuse for what they did.

The next time they were out of Jacob's sight, they grabbed Joseph, tore off his colourful coat, and dropped him down a dry well. They were just about to kill him, in fact, when they spotted a cloud of dust at the edge of the hill. It was a band of traders bound for Egypt, their camels loaded with goods for sale.

'Why should we kill Joseph,' asked one of the brothers, 'when we can sell him to these traders and make some money for ourselves? He'll be sold as a slave in Egypt and his foolish dreams will never come true!'

Twenty pieces of silver. That's how much the traders gave them for Joseph. And when the traders had gone, the brothers ripped up Joseph's coat, dipped it in the blood of a goat, and carried it home to their father.

'Joseph is dead,' they told Jacob. And they showed him Joseph's coat, its long sleeves shredded, its beautiful colours smeared with blood.

Jacob wept and wept.

And Joseph wept, too, as the traders carried him far from home.

Joseph the Prisoner

When the traders took Joseph to Egypt, they sold him to one of the king's own soldiers— a man named Potiphar. He was kind, and Joseph worked very hard for him. So hard, in fact, that Potiphar put Joseph in charge of all his other slaves.

Potiphar's wife, however, was evil and cruel. She told lies about Joseph and had him thrown in prison!

Things looked bad for Joseph. It seemed as if his dreams would never come true. But God was watching over him.

One morning, one of the other prisoners said, 'I had a dream last night. A strange dream. I dreamed I saw a grapevine with three branches. Suddenly, bunches of grapes burst out of those branches. So I squeezed them into a cup and gave it to the king to drink. I wonder what it means?'

Joseph listened to the dream. God listened, too. Then he whispered the dream's meaning into Joseph's ear.

'I know what it means!' said Joseph. 'Before you were sent to prison you served wine to the king. Well, in three days, you will be set free and serve him wine once more.'

That's exactly what happened. And when the wine-server was set free, he promised to help Joseph get out, too.

Two long years went by. Then, one morning, the king of Egypt said, 'I had a dream last night. A strange dream! And I can't work out what it means.'

'A dream?' said his wine-server. 'I know a man who can tell you all about your dreams.'

And straight away Joseph was brought from the prison.

'I was standing on the banks of the river,' the king told Joseph, 'when I saw seven fat cows walk up out of the water. They were chewing happily on the grass when seven other cows joined them. These cows were bony and thin, and, instead of eating the grass, they ate the first seven cows. But they stayed as skinny as ever! What can it mean?'

God whispered in Joseph's ear. Joseph listened. Then he bowed and said, 'Your Majesty, for the next seven years Egypt will grow many good crops and be as fat as those first cows. But after that, for another seven years, hardly any food at all will grow. So unless you want your people to look like those skinny cows, you must store up food in the good years and use it wisely later.'

The king was so impressed with Joseph's answer that he not only let him stay out of prison, he put him in charge of storing and saving and serving out Egypt's food.

Seven good years *were* followed by seven bad. And, after the king, Joseph became the most important man in Egypt. It was like a dream come true!

Joseph the Ruler

One day there was a knock at Joseph's door. And when he answered it, his eleven brothers were standing there!

They bowed down before him. They kissed his feet. And they begged, 'Kind sir, we have come to Egypt all the way from the land of Canaan. We have no food. We are starving. May we please buy some from you?'

Joseph said nothing. He just stared at his brothers. He knew who they were, but they did not recognize him.

'All right,' said Joseph, in his sternest voice. 'I will sell you food.' And he ordered his servants to load his brothers' animals.

But that wasn't all he told them to do. 'Take one of my silver cups,' he said, 'and hide it in the sack of food tied to the youngest lad's donkey.' Joseph had a plan. He wanted to see if his brothers had changed.

When Joseph's brothers reached the edge of the city, his servants stopped them and searched through their sacks. What did they find? The silver cup, of course!

'We don't know how it got there!' the brothers explained to Joseph.

'Your brother stole it, that's how,' Joseph answered. 'So he must stay here in Egypt and be my slave.'

'No, please,' begged the brothers. 'That would break our father's heart. Keep one of us, instead.'

When Joseph heard that, he knew his brothers had changed. So he told them who he was, right then and there.

'I am Joseph,' he announced, 'your long-lost brother.'

This news did not make his brothers feel any better. They were so frightened, in fact, that they could hardly speak.

'Don't be afraid,' said Joseph, 'I forgive you. You meant to hurt me, but God used what you did to save us all from this terrible famine. Now, go. Fetch my father and the rest of our family to come and live in Egypt with me.'

The brothers looked up.

The brothers grinned.

The brothers cheered!

And after a lot of hugging and hello-ing and handshaking, they set off for Canaan to tell Jacob the good news.

And Joseph? Joseph just sat back on his throne and smiled. And thanked God for making his dreams come true.

The Secret Baby

There was a basket in the water.

There was a baby in the basket!

The baby's big sister was watching from the river-bank.

And God was watching, too.

Why was the basket in the water?

Why was the baby in the basket?

Because the baby was a Hebrew—a great, great, great grandson of Abraham, Isaac, and Jacob.

'There are too many Israelites in Egypt,' the king said to his soldiers. 'If we are not careful, there will soon be more of them than of us! So I want you to kill every baby Hebrew boy.'

Some Hebrew mothers cried.

Some Hebrew mothers ran.

But this baby's mother was clever.

She covered a basket with tar—so it would not sink.

She laid her baby in the basket—and prayed that he would be quiet.

And she hid the basket in the reeds near the river-bank and hoped no one would notice.

But someone did.

And not just *any* someone. The daughter of the king himself!

She went to the river to bathe.

She spotted the basket boat.

She sent her servant to fetch it out.

And when she looked into it—oh, what a surprise!

The baby's big sister hid her eyes. She could not bear to watch.

But God kept watching. He had special plans for this baby.

'I don't care if this baby is a Hebrew,' the king's daughter announced. 'I want to keep him. Coochie-coochie-coo. I shall call him Moses. But I will need a serving woman to feed him and look after him . . .'

And that's when God nudged the baby's big sister, just enough so she'd jump up from where she'd been hiding.

'A serving woman?' she shouted, almost before she thought. 'I know a serving woman who can help you.'

'Well, then fetch her, girl,' commanded the princess.

And God just smiled. For now little Moses would be raised by his own mother, taught the Hebrew ways, and be ready for that day when God would use him to set his people free.

The Burning Bush

The sun was
burning hot.
Moses' skin
was burned
dark brown.
And suddenly,
he saw it—a
bright red
burning bush!
Its branches
crackled
orange and
red, and Moses
could not help but
watch—for the bush
did not burn up!
'Take off your
shoes,' came a voice from the bush. 'This is a very special place.'

'Who are you?' asked Moses. 'And why are you talking to me? I am just a poor shepherd.'

'I am the God of Abraham, Isaac, and Jacob—the God of Israel,' the voice replied. 'And you are more than a shepherd. You are Moses, the man I have chosen to lead my people out of Egypt.'

'I can't do that,' Moses trembled. 'I left Egypt years ago, and I'm an old man now.'

'You can do it. You must do it,' God answered, 'for my people are slaves in Egypt and have prayed to be set free. I have heard their prayers, and you are the man I have chosen.'

'But what if I go and they don't believe you sent me?' Moses asked.

'Take the walking stick that's in your hand,' God said, 'and throw it on the ground.'

Moses did as God told him—and the stick turned into a wriggling snake!

'Now pick it up,' God commanded.

Moses wrapped a shaking hand around the snake's scaly middle—and it turned back into a stick!

'Show them that!' God laughed. 'Then they'll believe you.'

'But I'm so shy,' Moses continued. 'I'm no good at talking to people.'

'Don't worry about that,' God assured him. 'Your brother Aaron loves to talk. You can take him with you. Now, go! My people need your help.'

So Moses went. He put on his shoes. He picked up his walking stick. And he went— off to set God's people free.

The Great Escape

Moses and Aaron went to visit the king of Egypt.

'God wants you to set his people free,' they announced.

But the king just laughed. 'Don't be silly,' he said. 'They do what I tell them. They work for nothing. I will never set them free.'

'Then I must warn you,' said Moses, 'God will make some very bad things happen until you change your mind.'

It started almost at once. The rivers of Egypt filled with blood. The houses of Egypt swarmed with frogs. The dust of Egypt turned into gnats.

But the king would not let God's people go.

The people in Egypt were covered with flies. The animals in Egypt grew sick and died. And ugly sores broke out on everyone.

But still the king would not let God's people go.

Hail pelted the land and broke down the crops. Locusts gobbled up what was left.

Then darkness like night fell for three whole days.

And still the king would not give in.

Finally, God sent an angel to kill the king's eldest son. And the eldest sons of the rest of the Egyptians.

Then, at last, the king said, 'Go! Go, and never come back!'

God's people cheered. God's people packed. God's people waved goodbye. But just as they reached the sea and were puzzling out how to get across, the king changed his mind!

He leaped into his chariot and led his army out after them. Soon, the sea stretched out before God's people and the Egyptian army rushed behind them like a wave. What could they do?

'Raise your special walking stick,' God whispered to Moses. And the sea split in two before them—leaving a path right down the middle! The people of Israel hurried along that path to the other side, the Egyptian army close behind. Just as the last of God's people had safely crossed, Moses lowered his stick, the waters rushed back, and the army was washed away.

God's people were free at last!

The Fall of Jericho

The walls of Jericho went round and round. Round and round the whole city. The walls were tall. The walls were thick. How would God's people ever get in?

Joshua's thoughts went round and round. Round and round inside his head. He was the leader of God's people now that Moses was dead. But how could he lead them into Jericho?

The sword of the Lord swung round and round. Round and round the angel's head. 'God will lead you into Jericho,' said the angel to Joshua. 'He has a secret plan. All you have to do is trust him.'

The soldiers of Israel gathered round and round. Round and round their leader, Joshua. He told them the angel's plan. He didn't leave out one bit. The soldiers were amazed!

So the army of Israel marched round and round. Round and round the walls of Jericho. Once round each day. Six days in a row. And the people of Jericho laughed.

'Why are they marching round and round? Round and round the walls of Jericho? Is this a parade? Is it some kind of trick? They'll never beat us this way!'

But when the army marched round and round, round and round on the seventh day—they marched round once, they marched round twice. They marched round Jericho seven times. Then they raised their voices. They blew their trumpets. And the walls came crashing down!

The people of Israel danced round and round. Round and round the ruins of Jericho. 'God is our helper!' they sang and they shouted. 'He will never let us down!'

David the Giant-Killer

Goliath was big.

He had to stoop to get through doorways. His head was always bumping up against the ceiling. And his friends thought twice before inviting him to dinner.

Goliath had a big spear. Ten feet long, at least. With a big iron point. And his big bronze armour weighed a hundred pounds or more.

Goliath had a big voice, too.

And, one day, he used it. He stamped out in front of his army and shouted across the valley to the soldiers camped on the other side.

'I am Goliath!' he bellowed. 'And I dare any of you to come and fight me. Win the fight, and we will be your slaves. Lose, and you must work for us.'

David was little.

Just a boy, really, who looked after the sheep. When he wanted a break from that, he carried cheese to his brothers in the army. And that's what he was doing one day, when he heard Goliath shout.

David was a little angry.

'Who does that giant think he is?' huffed David. 'Doesn't he know that the Lord God

himself watches over us? Why, with God's help, even I could beat that bully.'

So David took a little walk. He went to see the king.

'I want to fight the giant,' he announced.

And the king almost fell off his throne.

'But you are so little,' said the king. 'And he is so big!'

'A lion is big,' answered David. 'And so is a bear. But when they came after my sheep, the Lord God helped me face them and fight them off. He will do the same with this giant.'

'All right,' the king agreed. 'But at least let me lend you my armour.'

The armour was big. Too big. And so heavy that David could hardly move.

So he gave it back. And picked up five little stones instead. And a sling. And his trusty shepherd's staff.

Goliath gave a big laugh when he saw the little shepherd boy.

And he took two big steps.

David ran a little way.

Two more giant steps for Goliath.

And David ran a little further.

They were in the middle of the valley now, and everything was quiet.

Goliath roared a big roar, sucked in a big breath of air, and raised his big spear.

David sneaked his little hand into his little pouch, pulled out a little stone, and slipped it in his sling. Then he spun it round his head and let it fly.

And before the giant could say another word, the stone struck him on the head, and he fell with a big thud to the ground.

David's side shouted a big 'Hooray!'

Goliath's side whispered, 'Uh-oh.'

And from then on, some pretty big things happened to the little shepherd boy. He was given a king's reward. He was promised the hand of the king's daughter. And, one day, he became king himself! The very best king God's people ever had.

God Sends Fire

If David was the best king God's people ever had, then Ahab was one of the worst!

He didn't listen to the Lord God at all.

No, he worshipped a statue called Baal. And, what is worse, he made a lot of God's people do the same.

God was watching this, of course. And he was not happy that his people had forgotten him and had replaced him with a god who was nothing more than a pile of stones.

So he whispered into the ear of Elijah, a man who had not forgotten him.

'Elijah,' God whispered, 'tell King Ahab that what he is doing is wrong. Tell him that I will stop the rain from falling until he stops worshipping Baal.'

Elijah swallowed hard and passed God's message on to Ahab. But Ahab only laughed. That is, until it stopped raining.

One year went by.

Another year followed.

And there was not one drop of rain.

So, in the third year, Elijah went to see King Ahab again.

'Elijah, you trouble-maker!' Ahab roared. 'See what you have done! The crops have died. The wells are dry. And it's *all* your fault!'

'No, Your Majesty,' said Elijah. 'The fault is yours, for you have not obeyed the Lord God.'

'The Lord God—ha!' snapped Ahab. 'I don't have to listen to what he says. I follow Baal.'

'All right, then,' answered Elijah. 'Why don't we have a contest—to prove once and for all who the true God really is?'

And so they did—on the top of Mount Carmel, overlooking the sea. Elijah, prophet of the Lord God, stood on one side. Four hundred and fifty prophets of Baal stood on the other. And the people of Israel gathered around the bottom to watch.

The prophets of Baal went first. They stacked up a pile of wood. They killed a bull and laid it on the top. Then they prayed to Baal, and asked him to set the whole thing on fire. They prayed hard. They prayed long—from breakfast to lunchtime. But there was no fire. Not even a spark.

Elijah couldn't resist having a little fun. 'Perhaps Baal is asleep,' he joked. 'Or day-dreaming, or on holiday! Or maybe he's just a little hard of hearing.'

And so Baal's prophets prayed louder. But it made no difference, and by the middle of the afternoon they were exhausted.

And that's when Elijah took his turn. He piled up twelve stones—one for each of the sons of Jacob. He laid wood on top of that, then the bull. Finally he poured water over the whole thing!

The crowd was amazed. How would it ever catch fire?

But Elijah knew just what he was doing. 'Lord,' he prayed, 'you are the real God. Please show that to your people now, so they will follow you again.'

Elijah had barely opened his eyes when it happened. God sent fire from heaven that burned up not only the bull, but the water, stones and wood, as well!

'The Lord is God!' the people shouted.

Then they cheered for Elijah, chased away the prophets of Baal, and ran for cover. Because, suddenly, it had started to rain!

Jonah the Groaner

Jonah was a groaner.

That's right—a groaner.

So when God told him to go to Nineveh and tell the people who lived there to change their evil ways, what did Jonah do?

Jonah groaned.

'Not Nineveh!' he groaned. 'Anywhere but Nineveh. The people who live there are our enemies!'

And when he had stopped groaning, Jonah bought himself a ticket. A ticket for a boat ride. A boat ride that would take him far away from Nineveh.

God listened to Jonah groan. God watched him buy his ticket. But God still wanted Jonah to go to Nineveh.

So when the boat reached the deepest part of the sea, God sent a storm.

'God, help us!' cried a sailor. 'We're sinking!'

'God, save us!' cried another. 'We're tipping over!'

'God must be very angry,' cried the captain, 'with someone here on board.'

And what did Jonah do? Jonah groaned.

'It's me,' Jonah groaned. 'I'm the one God's angry with. He told me to go to Nineveh, and here I am, sailing in the opposite direction. Throw me into the sea and your troubles will be over.'

'God, forgive us!' the sailors cried as they tossed Jonah into the water. And almost at once, the sea grew calm.

'Oh dear,' Jonah groaned, 'I'm sinking.'

'Oh no,' Jonah groaned, 'I'm going to drown.'

'Oh my,' Jonah groaned, 'that's the biggest fish I've ever seen!'

And before he could groan another groan, the fish opened its mouth and swallowed Jonah up!

It was God who sent the fish—to rescue Jonah, and to give him time to think. He had plenty to groan about, of course—the fish's slimy stomach, the seaweed, the smell. But Jonah was still alive—and that was something to cheer about! So Jonah stopped his groaning and prayed a prayer:

'I was sinking, Lord. I was drowning. But you saved me. So now I will do whatever you want.'

Three days later, the fish spat Jonah up on a beach. And Jonah kept his promise—he went straight to Nineveh and told the people that God wanted them to change their evil ways.

'Forty days is all you've got,' he warned them. 'And if you haven't changed by then, God will destroy your city.'

The people of Nineveh listened. The people of Nineveh wept. Then the people of Nineveh changed! From the king right down to the poorest slave, they decided to do what was right.

And what did Jonah do? Jonah groaned. He sat himself down in the shadow of a tree, and he groaned.

'I knew this would happen,' he groaned. 'You are a loving God who loves to forgive. But I still don't like the people of Nineveh and I wish they had been destroyed.'

Jonah fell asleep, groaning. And during the night, God sent a worm to kill the tree. When Jonah awoke, he groaned more than ever.

'The tree is dead!' he groaned. 'And now I have no shade.'

'Oh, Jonah,' God sighed. 'You cry about this tree, but you care nothing for the people of Nineveh. I want you to love them like I do.'

'And finally,' God added, 'I want you to stop your groaning!'

Daniel and the Lions

God was very sad. Most of his people had stopped listening to him, and talking to him, and following his rules.

'If you do not change your ways,' he warned them, 'you will have to leave this special country I gave you long ago.'

But the people would not listen. So God let their enemies defeat them, and destroy their cities, and carry them hundreds of miles away to be slaves in another land.

There were, however, a few of God's people who did not forget him. One of them was Daniel.

He worked hard in the new land—so hard that he became one of the king's own helpers! But he never forgot about God, or failed to pray to him, morning, noon and night.

Some of the king's men were jealous of Daniel. They wanted his job for themselves. So they talked the king into making a new law, a law which said, 'No one, but no one, is allowed to pray to anyone but the king himself.'

'We've got Daniel, now!' his enemies laughed.

And so they had. For the very next morning, Daniel knelt by his window, bowed his head and prayed—not to the king, but to God.

'Thank you for taking care of us in this faraway land,' he prayed. 'Forgive us, and please take us back to our own land, soon.'

Daniel's enemies were watching. And before he could even open his eyes, they grabbed him and dragged him in front of the king.

The king was sad. Very sad. He liked Daniel. But he could not break his own law.

'Daniel must be punished,' he sighed. 'Throw him into the lion pit.'

But even as the king gave the order, he whispered a prayer that no one could hear. A prayer to Daniel's God that, somehow, Daniel might be saved.

The pit was dark. The pit was deep. The lions covered its floor like a shaggy growling carpet. They leaped to their feet in a second when Daniel landed among them. They licked their lips. They showed their teeth. Their eyes shone bright and fierce. They opened their mouths and moved towards their dinner. And then they stopped.

'Shoo! Scat! Go away!' shouted a voice right behind Daniel.

The lions' mouths snapped shut. Their tails drooped. And they whimpered away to the corners of the cave.

Slowly Daniel turned around, and looked up into the face of an enormous angel!

'Nothing to worry about, now,' the angel smiled. 'God sent me to watch over you. Why don't you get some sleep?'

The next morning, the king cheered when he discovered that Daniel was still alive.

'Pull Daniel out,' he ordered his men. 'And while you're at it, take the men that talked me into that silly law and dump them into the pit instead.'

The king put his arm around Daniel and walked him back to the palace.

Meanwhile Daniel's enemies cried for help. And the lions enjoyed their breakfast!

Other Bob Hartman titles
from Lion Publishing:

New Testament Tales
from The Lion Storyteller Bible

The Lion Storyteller Bible

The Lion Storyteller Bedtime Book

Angels, Angels All Around

Cheer Up, Chicken!

Time to Go, Hippo!